T0368378

What Would You Do if This Were You?

Left by the Rapture

Lucille Langston

authorHOUSE®

AuthorHouse™
1663 Liberty Drive
Bloomington, IN 47403
www.authorhouse.com
Phone: 833-262-8899

This book is a work of non-fiction. Unless otherwise noted, the author and the publisher make no explicit guarantees as to the accuracy of the information contained in this book and in some cases, names of people and places have been altered to protect their privacy.

Published by AuthorHouse 11/26/2024

ISBN: 979-8-8230-3689-4 (sc)
ISBN: 979-8-8230-3688-7 (e)

Library of Congress Control Number: 2024923225

Print information available on the last page.

Any people depicted in stock imagery provided by Getty Images are models, and such images are being used for illustrative purposes only. Certain stock imagery © Getty Images.

Scripture taken from the King James Version of the Bible.

This book is printed on acid-free paper.

HEAVEN	HELL
❖ A man's back is turned; he's walking up a grand and heavenly staircase; wearing a long white gown; A heavenly look; a cross; bright shining light; People are wearing white gowns following and smiling.	❖ A man's back is turned; He is wearing all black; a fire is burning; the devil's pitchfork is present; people are following the man screaming and crying "No! No!

What happened to the people that were left behind during the rapture?

What benefit does a non-believer have when he/she realizes that God is going to judge us and that He holds the keys- eternal Heaven or Hell?

God encourage me to encourage people that there's a real Heaven and Hell and that we have to choose where we want to spend eternal life.

This film will make you think a little bit. A light should come on inside your head and make you wonder. Pay close attention and I think you will learn something from this movie, whether you believe in God or not.

Before the rapture took place, God had to reveal, to some of these characters, why they were left behind. Pay close attention to these characters to determine whether you are making the same mistake(s) and what you need to do to fix these mistakes before it is too late. There are several characters whom God had been dealing with. He was not pleased with this. These characters are ones who stood out before the rapture-the ones God had been dealing with.

Beginning of the Movie

Man: I am a pastor who preaches and sings well. Then, I go home and beat my wife.

Woman: I practiced witchcraft on a woman for cheating with my husband. The wife visited the hospital to see the cheating woman sick. The cheating woman asked the wife to forgive her and then asked God the same. The wife would not issue forgiveness.

Teenager (boy/girl): I am 18 years old. I disrespect my mother, drink, and use drugs. The bad crowd came to get him/her that night, but the bad crowd got in trouble and God spared the child as he took a shower to join the crowd. The bad crowd left him.

Man/Woman(Selfish and Negative person): I like hurting people, seeing them fail, and trapping them.

Saul: I do not like Christian; I will have you murdered. Saul does not believe in Jesus Christ.

There was a loud noise- an airplane crashing, an earthquake, and a burning crop. Animals were dying. Everything was going bad. The Christians who were rapture-ready disappeared. The abusive pastor, the witchcraft-practicing wife, the unruly 18-yr old, the selfish and negative person, and Saul were all left behind. God was trying to get their attention. However, they were too involved and caught up on themselves. These are just some of the characters who stood out- for the purpose of showing why they were left behind.

*Matthew 24:44 Therefore you also be ready, for the Son of man is coming at an hour you will not expect.

*Exodus 20:3 Thou shalt have no other gods before me.

I Am The Pastor

Today is Sunday. I am in church singing and preaching my heart out. My family- wife and children- is in the audience. Sunday service was perfect. We greeted and fellowshipped with one another. While the rest of my family continued to mingle, I fellowshipped with my mistress. She didn't want to see me anymore, because she's, now, found GOD. He sent her a soulmate to marry. (The pastor tells her to leave his office. The pastor comes out of his study and leaves with his wife and children. The pastor gets home. The pastor asked his wife, "Why is it so hard for you to lose weight? God made me head and you need to look like I want you to look!" The wife says "Baby I am trying! I love you!" (She tried to kiss him and he knocked her down). The pastor says, "You don't love me because I asked you, good, to lose weight and you are still fat!" (At that time, the rapture took place.)

Pastor: My wife was raptured, but I was left.

I Am the Witchcraft Woman

One Saturday night, my husband said that he must go to a meeting. He kissed me and said that he loved me. He told me to keep the bed warm. I knew he was cheating because when he came home, he'd often accuse me of cheating. His guilty conscience was getting the best of him. Instead of me seeking revenge against him, I wanted to reprimand the woman, which was wrong. I was so in love with my husband, I believed everything he told me. I knew where the woman lived, and I knew who she was. My husband held a picture of her in his wallet. I retrieved the picture from his wallet. He had no clue. I got her picture and other items to make her sick. As a result, she had to seek medical attention.

I knew her every move. I visited the hospital and confronted this woman, asking "Why were you cheating with my husband?" (She responded that God had forgiven her and asked the wife to forgive her as well.)

Witchcraft Woman: If you cheat with my husband, again, I will make you sick like this again and again.

Mistress (Sick Woman): I have learned my lesson.

When the raptured appeared, the sick lady was raptured because she had asked of God's forgiveness and had asked the Witchcraft woman for forgiveness as well. She (The witchcraft woman) and her husband were, both, left behind. Her husband scolded her and said, "Your witchcraft is your god!"

Scripture- Exodus 20:3- Thou shalt have no other gods before me

Witchcraft Woman: My husband and I repented and when God comes back, we will be ready to go to Heaven.

I Am the Disobedient 18-year Old

I disrespect my parents. I smoke, drink, and hang with a bad crowd. One Saturday night, my so-called friend called me on the telephone to tell me how we could make some good money.

Disobedient Teen: What do we have to do?

So-Called Friend: Man, you ask too many questions! Are you going or not?!- Look! They are expecting us to be there ASAP! Are you going or not- with your broke self!

Disobedient Teen: I am going because I need the money.

So-called Friend: You don't know when God is trying to bless you (Only to trick his friend)! (Hangs up the phone)

The so-called friend jumped in his car to pick up all of his friends (including the disobedient teen). Once he got to the last house to pick up a friend, he began to blow his horn and even knock on the friend's door- no answer. This particular friend, God had been working on and attempting to get their attention. They were in the shower the entire time.

I am The Selfish and Negative Person

I enjoy hurting people. I enjoy seeing them fail.

I am at my office working one Monday afternoon. I am the boss. I have men and women working for me- one, in particular, has been with me for quite some time and is hard-working and dedicated. On the other hand, there is a new guy. He came to work for me because he and I are close friends- buddies. He can, pretty much, do anything he wants for that reason, alone. Other workers will not get this privilege and some I will pick on because they are either not as smart as me, don't drive the car that fits my style, or are in a living situation below my standards. I am above them and they are beneath me. I am better than those low-class folks. Honestly, I laid off a good worker so my friend could have a job. After all, his family needs the money. I don't care about the other worker or what his needs are- their problem, not mine.

All of a sudden, the company shut down. The mean and hateful character was, eventually, forced to move into a shelter.

Mean and Hateful Person: This is what I found out that we all know what we do wrong and, most of all, God knows. We try to pretend, but we are only fooling ourselves.

When God came back for his church, I was not ready

to go with him because I had not repented of my sins

SCRIPTURE- Proverbs 16:18 "Pride goeth before

destruction, and a haughty spirit before a fall."

I Am Saul

I am Saul. I do not like real Christians. I have my own setup in place. My set up does not require followers to abide by all the bible rules. My place is all together. We are all very well groomed and educated. We look good and drive the finest cars. I give good money all the time and know that my money will make up for all of my wrong-doing. People love coming to my place because they have the freedom to do what ever it is that they want to do. I tell them to come to *me* and I can forgive them. I also encourage them to give a large donation which will cover them.

Once, I had a family to come to my establishment. They explained that they had come to find "our Lord and Savior, Jesus Christ."

Saul: *resentfully* Why does it have to be all of that- way too much information; way too many words! Let's try that again.

Male Family Member: What do you want us to say?

Saul: *boastfully* Say you have come to be a servant to me!

Male Family Member: We have come to serve Jesus Christ.

Saul, immediately, summoned some of his staff to escort the family away to be killed. (Exodus 20:13 Thou shall not kill.) The congregation looked on, wondering what would happen to the family. After that the meeting was over and everyone left the building- everyone except Saul. He went to his office where he was met by one of God's angels. Once he understood that the presence of God was upon him, he listened.

Saul: Lord, what will you have me to do?

Angel of the Lord: (Acts 2:38) Repent and be baptized, every one of you, in the name of Jesus Christ for the forgiveness of your sins. And you will receive the gift of the Holy Spirit.

I Am God's Messenger

There was a place in a cave designated as a meeting ground for people interested in knowing about God. In attendance were complete non-believers and others who had heard about God, but who had not tried Him and were not sure who He is.

For some reason, unknown to them, they were led to this cave. God's messenger let the people know that the rapture had taken place and that their loved ones were saved and during the Rapture went back with God.

God's Messenger: If you want to go to Heaven to be with your loved ones, you must be born again!

He shared a few scriptures to communicate the urgency of the actions that must take place on their part.

The Rapture

Guards and police are patrolling on their daily duties. The world does not know what is about to take place...

The rapture has happened.

Mark 13:22 For false christs and false prophets shall rise and shall shew signs and wonders to seduce, if it were possible, even the elect.

During this time, the antichrist followers had called a secret meeting to discuss how to gather the people who were left on Earth. The plan was to deceive them and convince them to receive "the mark" to survive. This mark would be exhibited on their forehead or right hand. The mark was of the antichrist (devil) and would ensure followers a trip to hell. The antichrist tried his best to trick the people, telling them that the mark would, even, make their lives better.

The followers and his team tried many ways to deceive the people- with other men and women; money; cars; authority/power and great jobs. The false prophets claimed to be able to prosper people.

Revelations 13:13 And he doeth great wonders, so that he maketh fire come down from heaven on the earth in the sight of men.

*Read your bible and pay close attention so that you won't be deceived by any means.

I Am God's Messenger (cont.)

While God's messenger was in the cave talking, people were still coming, running for their lives. Everything was dying- the land, animals, etc. Everything was going bad. Police and military were everywhere. Someone overheard talking about one name Balaam and how he is supposed to fix everything. However, Balaam is the antichrist's name.

Mark 13:22 For false christs and false prophets shall rise, and shall shew signs and wonders, to seduce, if it were possible, even the elect.

Revelations 13:13 And he doeth great wonders,so that he maketh fire come down from Heaven on the earth in the sight of men.

Daniel 12:11 And from the time that the daily sacrifice shall be taken away, and the abomination that maketh desolate set up, there shall be a thousand two hundred and ninety days.

Matthew 24:21 [21] For then shall be great tribulation, such as was not since the beginning of the world to this time, no, nor ever shall be.

This was a time on Earth not safe for anyone. This was the time of tribulation.

Mark 13:17 But woe to them that are with child and to them that give suck in those days!

Revelation 6:12 [12] **And I beheld when he had opened the sixth seal, and, lo, there was a great earthquake; and the sun became black as sackcloth of hair, and the moon became as blood;**

Revelation 8:9 And the third part of the creatures which were in the sea, and had life, died; and the third part of the ships were destroyed.

Revelation 13:15 And he had power to give life unto the image of the beast, that the image of the beast should both speak, and cause that as many as would not worship the image of the beast should be killed.

God's Messenger (repeating): If you want to go to Heaven where your loved are, you must be born again. There is no time to waste!

Luke 13:3 I tell you, Nay: but, except ye repent, ye shall all likewise perish.

Example Prayer: Dear Heavenly Father,

I am coming to you as humble as I know how. I am asking You to forgive me for all my sins and come into my life and save me and keep me. Amen.

John 3:3 Jesus answered and said unto him, Verily, verily, I say unto thee, Except a man be born again, he cannot see the kingdom of God.

Romans 10:9-10 That if thou shalt confess with thy mouth the Lord Jesus, and shalt believe in thine heart that God hath raised him from the dead, thou shalt be saved.

[10] For with the heart man believeth unto righteousness; and with the mouth confession is made unto salvation.

1st Thessalonians 4:16 For the Lord himself shall descend from heaven with a shout, with the voice of the archangel, and with the trump of God: and the dead in Christ shall rise first:

2nd Corinthians 5:10 For we must all appear before the judgment seat of Christ; that everyone may receive the things done in his body, according to that he hath done, whether it be good or bad.

While God's messenger was still in the cave discussing and explaining information the refugees needed to know, the antichrist followers called a meeting. There, they instructed army men and police to be on guard and to ensure that every person they encountered had been branded with "the mark" on their forehead or right hand. People were not allowed to buy, sell, or be seen, for that matter, without this mark. If you were caught without the mark, you had 2 options: 1) Receive the mark or 2) Get beheaded (which ensured an automatic entrance into Heaven).

The antichrist followers are, now, telling the people that things will get better since they have the mark and with the help of Balaam. Now the antichrist follower is about to introduce his god, Balaam- the antichrist.

2nd Thessalonians 2:4 Who opposeth and exalteth himself above all that is called God, or that is worshipped; so that he as God sitteth in the temple of God, shewing himself that he is God

Antichrist Follower: Father, Balaam, tell the crowd we've come to make peace and not war.

Balaam tells them to trust him (they shouldn't). He would never lie to them. (He will) He tells them third temple has been set up for them to worship together. He tells them that they should follow him and this will be like paradise on Earth! Together they will eliminate the burnt offering in the temple and enjoy the good life that he has promised them.

Daniel 12:11; And from the time that the daily sacrifice shall be taken away, and the abomination that maketh desolate set up, there shall be a thousand two hundred and ninety days.

2nd Thessalonians 2:4

Who oppeseth and exalteth himself above all that is called God, or that is worshipped; so that he as God sitteth in the temple of God, shewing himself that he is God

Balaam (cont.): He tries to convince them he's the answer to their problems. They can depend on him. If they need the mark, see his follower. We cannot survive without the mark!

Sadly, people who did not know Christ took the mark, immediately. Others, who had heard about the antichrist, and were on the run for their lives, refused to do so. Families and friends turned on one another. Some people were beheaded. A husband left his pregnant wife behind because she could not keep up.

Sadly, people who did not know Christ took the mark, immediately. Others, who had heard about the antichrist, and were on the run for their lives, refused to do so. Families and friends turned on one another.

Some people were beheaded. A husband left his pregnant wife behind because she could not keep up.

Antichrist Follower (to the husband): We need someone like you. You left your wife behind because she hindered you! The antichrist honors his followers. We need people like you! Trust us!

Antichrist: Antichrist tells them they will be honored with great things! Name it and it's theirs! All they have to do is make sure everyone they encounter has the mark. If they do not and cannot be persuaded, cut their necks off! Then, the spirit of God showed up from the East in a great wind!

The antichrist and his followers continued their meeting.

The ground opened up, all of sudden, and swallowed the antichrist and his followers up in a lake of fire!

God gathered his children and went away. They were now in His presence.

The End

Printed in the United States
by Baker & Taylor Publisher Services